FINN'S FUN TRUCKS
FARM FLEET

Written by Finn Coyle   Illustrated by Srimalie Bassani

I'm Sandy the farmer. I run my farm with the help of some really awesome machines.

Each one has a job of its own.
Can you guess what each one does?

This is a
TRACTOR.
Can you guess what it does?

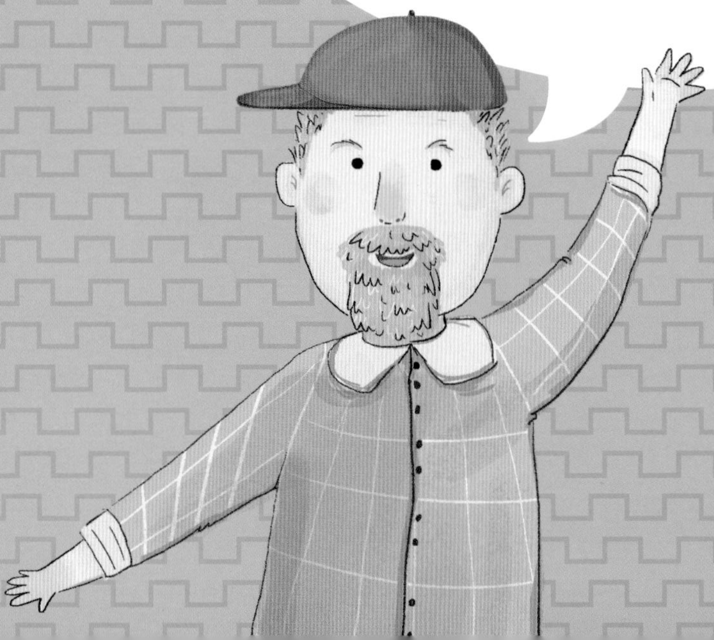

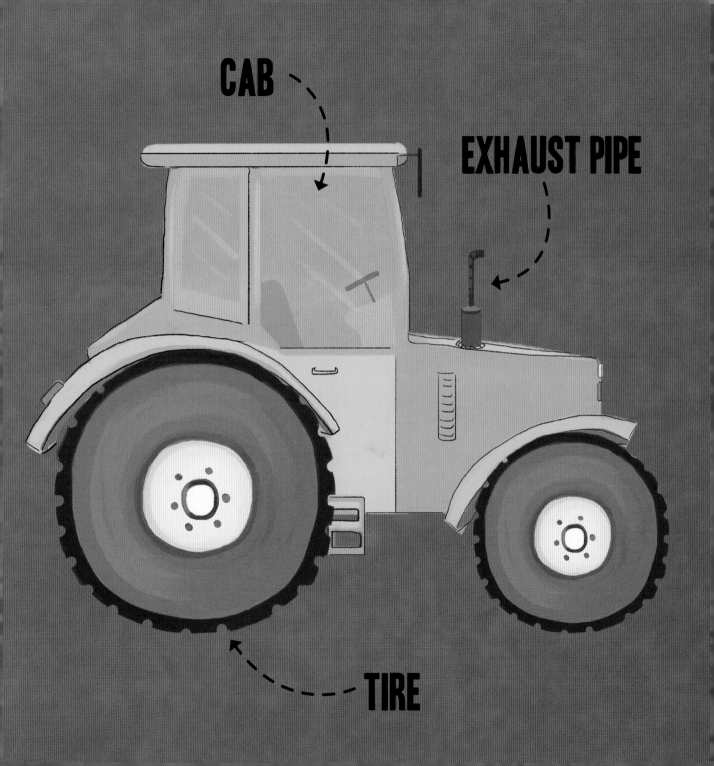

A tractor helps me move around the farm.
It can also pull a lot of my other machines.

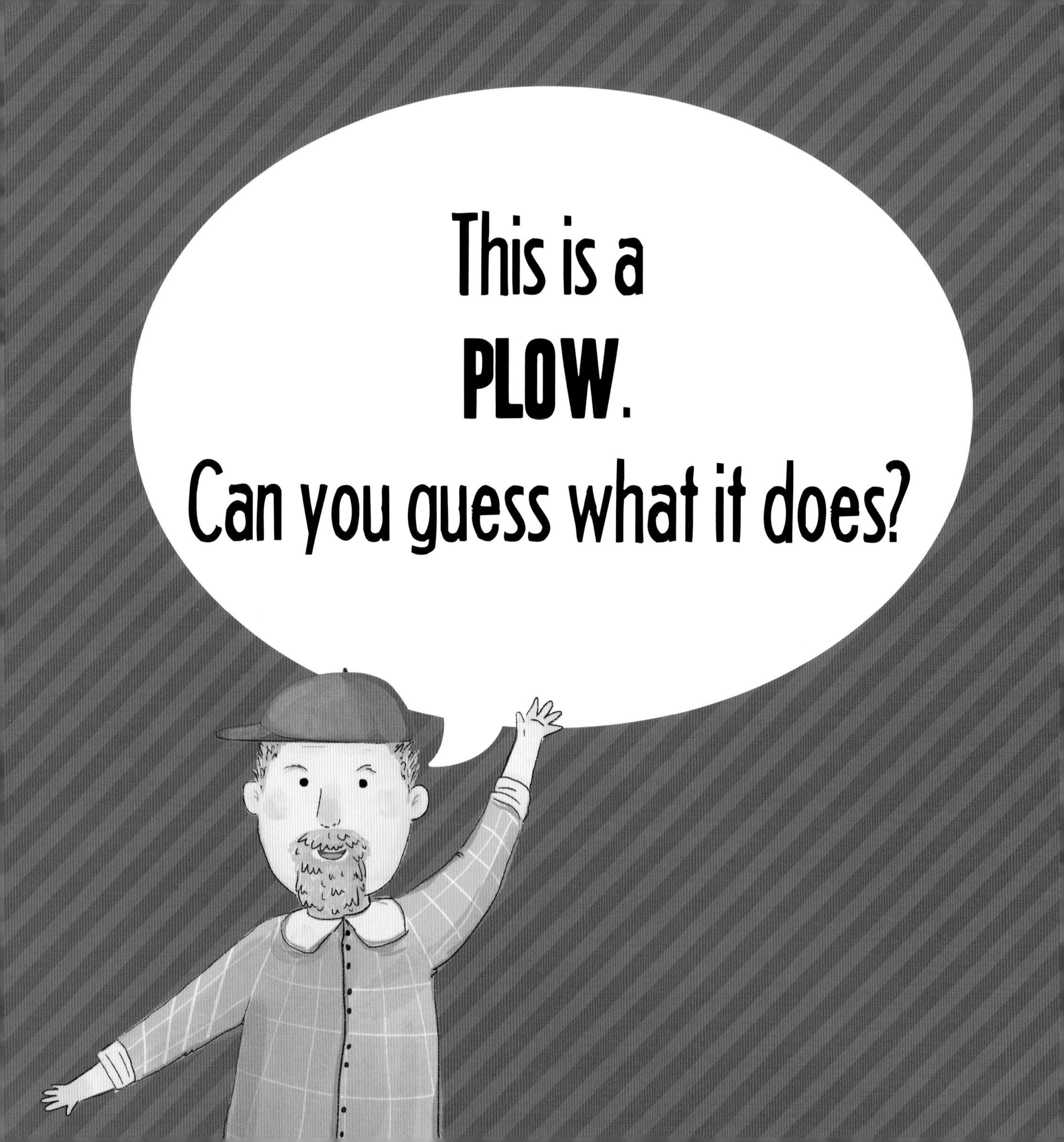
This is a
PLOW.
Can you guess what it does?

MAST

FRAME

MOLDBOARDS

A plow attaches to the back of a tractor. It turns the soil over so crops will grow tall and healthy.

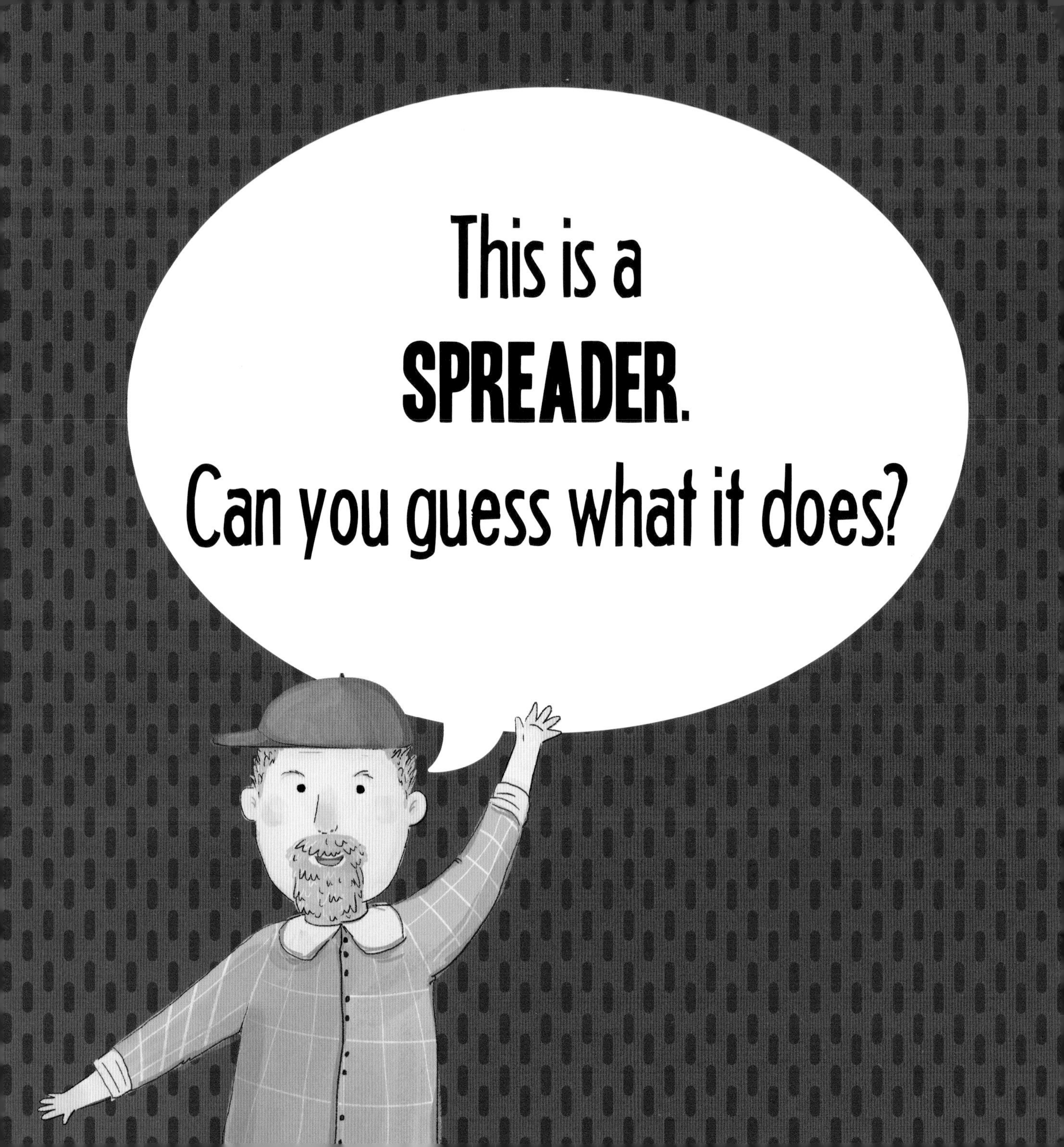
This is a
SPREADER.
Can you guess what it does?

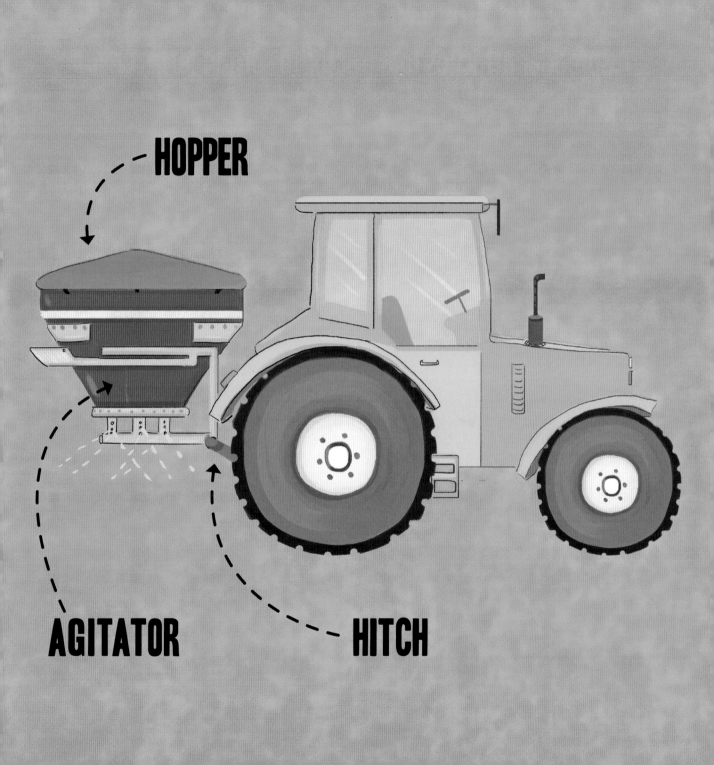

HOPPER

AGITATOR

HITCH

A spreader attaches to a tractor to spread fertilizer in the fields.

It can also feed the crops when they are young.

This is a
HARVESTER.
Can you guess what it does?

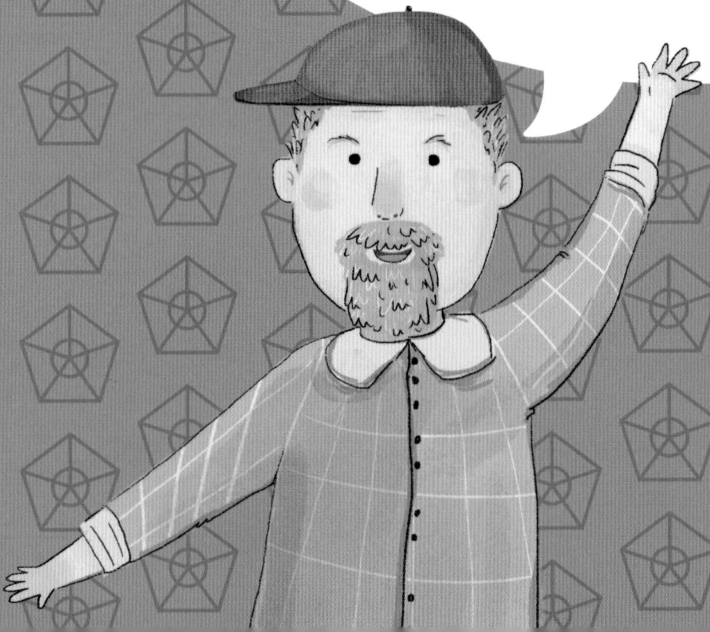

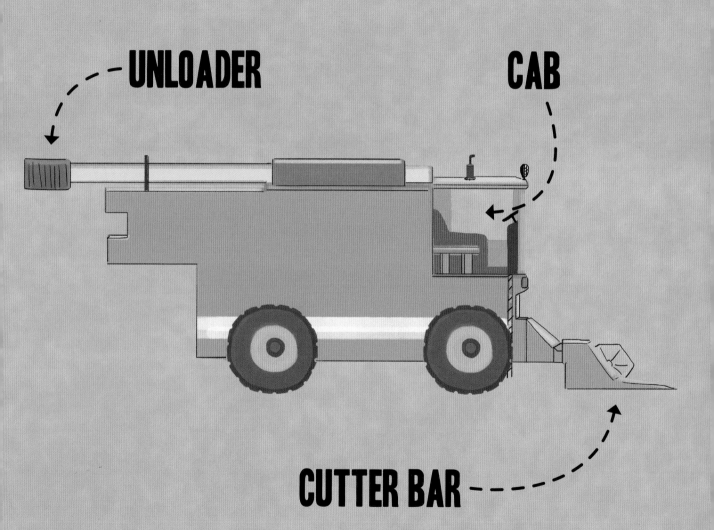

A harvester cuts down the crops when they are fully grown. It can also separate and collect the food from the rest of the plant.

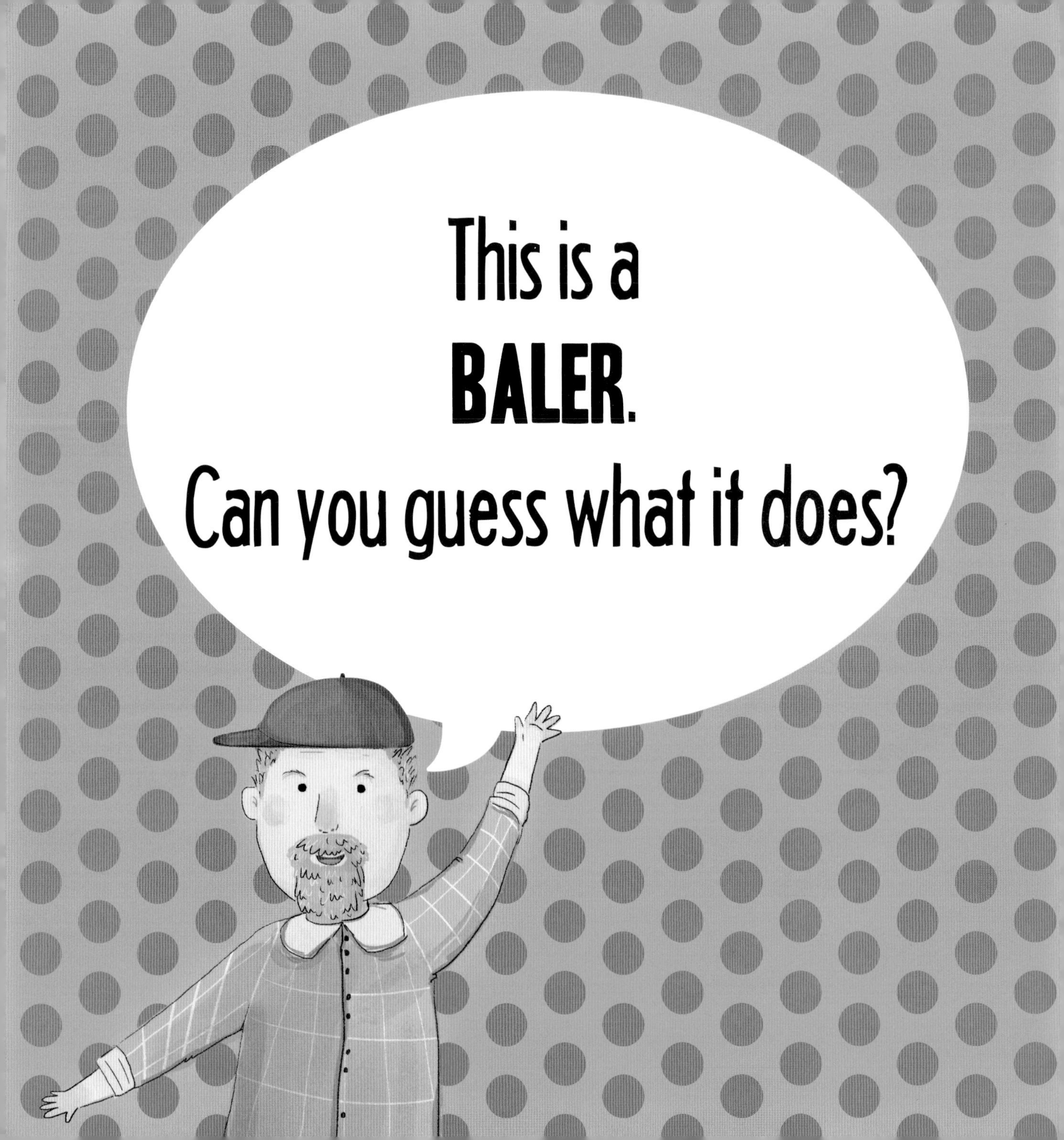
This is a
BALER.
Can you guess what it does?

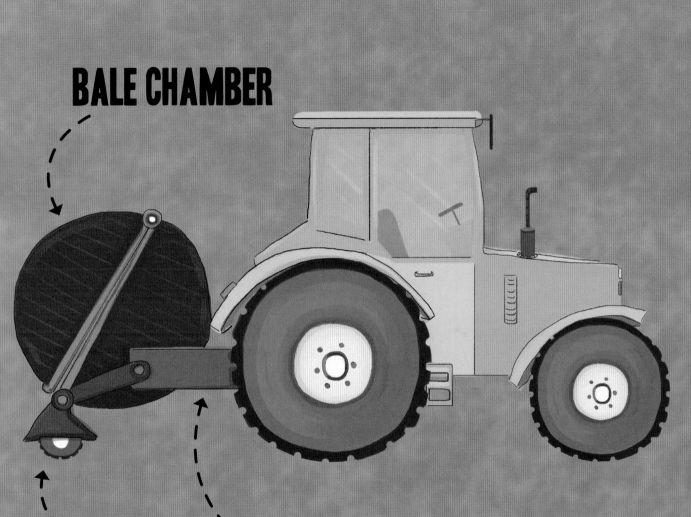

BALE CHAMBER

WHEEL **PICKUP**

A baler attaches to a tractor. It makes bales of hay that I can take to the barn to feed the animals.

This is my farm fleet!

Can you guess what they can do
when they all work together?

They can help me grow all kinds of great food!

TRACTOR

HARVESTER

SPREADER

BALER

PLOW